There Were Words

David Bowden

ISBN:
ISBN-13: 978-1482757224

Dedicated to two brides:
My lovely, supportive, and joyful wife,
and the everlasting, undying, universal bride of Christ

CONTENTS

A SHORT PREFACE

This is a compilation of some of my favorite works from the last four years. These poems were written to be performed out loud and not read in quiet. Therefore, I pray that you read these pages through the lens of the spoken word and hear the words with your eyes.

To God's glory, for the sake of His Son, through the power of His Holy Spirit, and for the building up of His church. Amen.

DEATH AND HIS STING

And I saw him
Death with his mighty sting
Exhaling in every breath the plight he brings
To the grave he gave victory
Triumphing over life with the fear of endless sleep
Endlessly we hide from our mortality
Mortally wounded from birth
We lie to ourselves from infancy
Infinitely investing time in a life
That will inevitably be taken by this
Incredible creature that stands before me:
Death

He manifests himself on ordinary days
His six-foot stomach growls with hunger pangs
For his meal, he cannot wait
So we are forced to taste him even before the grave
We are all dying, there is no other way

I see him in Haitian and Japanese earthquakes
He's hating the escapees of his cruel wakes

I see him in poverty
Impoverishing the quality of life
In regions that are reachable
And in those with the reach
Who find reason not to reach
Out to treat what is treatable

I see him in disease
Taking life out of uninfected
Yet affected families

I see him in oppression
Pressing down on the oppressed
And the oppressor

I see him in depression
In Prozac and pain pills
In razor blades and bedside wills

I see him in abuse
Physical, emotional, mental misuse

I see him in
Spiritual confusion
Material obsessions
Physical possessions

I see him in marital transgressions
Childhood remorse
From an ugly divorce

I see him in our slavery to appearances
Appearing to care more about our images
Than those in dying villages

I see him in our ignorance
Ignoring truth for some more comfortable inference

I see his emergence in our churches
As we pull out emergency verses as deterrents
To religious differences, going on the defensive
Defending our way of worship
Making community worthless

Death is killing us
Before we even enter the surface of the earth
We are in service to his words
"It is finished"
The end of our birth

We cannot escape his wretched curse
For Death and his grave we constantly rehearse

Even God Himself was coerced
Divinity immersed itself in humanity
Humbly taking on flesh, scorning vanity
The world saw His way of life as insanity
Insisting He cease speaking of this
Radical Christianity

But man found Him guilty
Accusing God of blasphemy
Performing the ultimate usurpation
By slaying Christ on Calvary

But through their cowardly cross
Jesus embossed mankind with amnesty
Championing over Death
With the beauty of His fatal injury

And I know
Many still doubt, and rightfully so
Bringing up this inquiry:

"What does that poor Jewish man
Dying on a Roman tree
2,000 years ago have to do with me?"

I reply simply:
Christ came and died to marry His bride to be
And though Death could kill the Groom
It could not kill the ring
God made us one with Christ and life
In matrimony's cling
Now the undying church
His ever-living wife can sing

"Oh Death, where is your sting?
Oh Grave, where is your victory?
For we have risen above your misery!
We will not succumb to your finality!
For have overcome your infamous mystery
In the infinite reign of Christ's ministry!"
For we are the resurrection
The insurrection of fatality
We are the risen deity
The intersection of a dead yet living body
We live through imperfections
For we died to become holy
We cannot be contained
By the mouth of the grave
We are the willing slaves
Of the One who rose
From the garden cave
We have passed through death to new birth
We gave the grave to the earth
And we claim today the cross's worth
The body of His rising
We are the risen church

DIVERSITY'S SYMPHONY

I was raised Southern Baptist
What I believed was what others practiced
A white church planted in red dirt
A Midwestern boy with a tucked in shirt

I converted not just to Christianity
But to an ideology, an identity
An idea, a theology
I was taught Jesus died for the sins of humanity
That His cross would demolish all hints of inequality
That He cried out for unity
At His last prayer at Gethsemane
And that this infallible book
Would bring all believers to harmony

But across the street
Were the Nazarenes
And two blocks down
Were the Catholics
And a mile north
A church called Community
And east of that
Were more Baptists

I had this un-calloused
Thought that if we couldn't have fellowship
With those in other fellowships
Who were taught a little different

Then we could at least befriend the Baptists
Who were baptized for the same reasons
And under the same creeds
And because of the same tree
But these Baptists weren't like the
Baptists in our baptistery washing away their sin
For though these Baptists shared our beliefs
They did not share our skin

We are born into a separated Sunday morning
The body of Christ
Is segregated past all warnings
The church looks more like a court
And less like a courting
Trading the unified bride for stereotype judgments
The juries are sorting
The blacks from the white
The left from the right
The women from men
The sinners from sin
The traditional from the charismatic
The liberal from the dogmatic
The denomination from the non-denom
Inevitably separating us from God

How did we get so far off from the truth
That now
A poor, dark skinned, unattractive, Israeli-Jew
Would have better luck dying for our sins
Than fitting in on our pews?

Are our views and traditions
Worth destroying the body of Christ's
Eternal commission
Baptizing all nations
Under the damnation
Of our denomination's fraternal omission?

We are omitting the ominous call to depart
From the social roles and charts
Our stratified cultures impart
But it's time our churches look less like
The demographic of a country club
And more like that of a Wal-Mart

Before the cross
All races and nations fit into two percentiles
God's chosen Israel and the un-chosen Gentiles
Those who could enter the temple
And those exiled by its walls
But after the cross
The hostility built into that divider did fall

And a new people were born
A holy nation set apart from all who'd lived before
Within this borderless country
There is no

Jew nor Gentile
Male nor female
Rich nor poor
Democrat nor Republican

Iraqi nor American
Homely nor beautiful
Polished nor tainted
Catholic nor Baptist
Red nor brown
Black nor white
There is only Christ
The miracle of a true life
The participants in the new creation
The old has gone the new has saved us
We are the third race
Neither Gentile nor Jew
From death to life we have all passed through
Our skin has not been removed
But our eyes have been renewed

Now you can see me and I can see you
As more than a brand, title, sinner, or color
But as a father, mother, sister, or brother

The church is universal, the university of diversity
She can teach the world how to live in harmony
The church is local, the locale for unity
Unifying heaven and earth
We are the contrasted community

Our allegiance is not to a country, color, or creed
But to the androgynous family born on that Roman
tree

We will no longer be separated
By our prejudices or bigotry
Nor be segregated
From those who think or look differently
But will embrace our body's beautiful diversity
And will raise our voices for peace
As God's extraordinary symphony

GOD'S VALENTINE

Upon the eve of Adam, deity rang an anthem
Sang an album
Banged a bass drum
For His love had begun

The heavens took aim
At loneliness, hate
Selfishness, and shame
His hands became
The battle lines
By creating planets for His valentine

He presented her with gardens of flowers
Mountainous towers of cards
Glistening seas of treats
And their date took place
Under the shade of the second night's stars
The garden wrapped with leaf and vine
The seventh day, first valentines

Then the lover penned a love note
Opened His ominous throat
He wrote transcendent quotes
That descended upon Sinai's mountain
This letter spoke of what the heaven's saw
How the creator stood in awe of creation
Raw revelation rested on humanity
Flaws and all

The law was scrawled out in drawl vowels
The lover's keeper of elated emotions ran
Deeper than His created oceans
Better than nature's wine, the law
Love's first written valentine

But His creation's devotion
Soon sank with the weight of their inflated notions
They berated His holiness
By degrading the homeless
Parading their boldness
Trading the memo of Moses
For a new soulless Pharaoh
Their own kings
Their own laws
Their own things
Their own gods
They broke the author's heart by building shrines
To what were meant to serve as signs
To the designer not the design
But His creation fell in love with creation's valentine

The lover tried to win back His bride
He bribed her when He described His
Love through His prophets
Emptied His pockets
Of profits and punishment
Sent more messengers than they could murder
To prove His fervor and commitment
But His love was met with nothing but fervent
resistance
No matter how hard He tried
They would always decline
His love littered valentine

But the lover resigned to
Restore His creation's design
He declined sending anymore
Lofty letters or mystical messages
He was inclined to heal Earth's damages
By leaving His palace
To deliver His cordate packages

The lover descended on His creation
Practicing His previous letters
Hand-delivering notes to the poor, blind, and lepers
Exposing the gloats of common temple dwellers
Explaining how giving up your cloak
Is a Godlike gesture
Examining the hope found in
Forgiving your debtors
Surrendering your pleasures
Redefining your treasures
Revealing that He was the sender
Of those ancient ancestral letters

Then
He composed one more note of love
He showed it, not from on high,
But with lowly blood
The lover wrote how much His love had cost
His pen was flesh dipped nails
His paper was a cross

On the feast of His offering
He called creation to dine
Receive peace through His suffering
The last valentine

Now that I have penned mine
I pass the ink to you
To create, as the creator
Love notes with what you do

Send them to family
But to your enemies too
Write out loud to those in poverty
Whom others see through
Use your own flesh's ink to keep the message true
And wear the lover's letters like a tattered tattoo

With an eternity of messages
From our love-struck divine
May we go forth into forever
His valiant valentines

NO EXCUSE

I write to you
Poets and martyrs
Disciples and daughters
Elders and brothers
Christians and lovers
Pastors and teachers
Prophets and preachers
I write to you
Leaders
That you might gather the weapons from your armories
Grab your pulpits and mics
Your stages and lights
Your buildings and pews
Your resources be used
For the wife has been bruised
Her body beaten and bludgeoned
She's cheated on the man she once pursued
For the bride has now forgotten her husband
I write to you for you have been summoned
That you might surrender
Your church services and your functions
Your evening worship and your luncheons
Bring your members by the dozens
No matter your shortcomings or dysfunctions
You have been summoned to bear this insistence
God wants to use every part of your existence
And none of you are any different

If your church is slowing or resurgent
Older or but an infant
You are part of the resistance
To stand your ground against
The armies of apathy that are rising against us

I write to you because
I see Christians, but I don't see Christ
I see people living, but not surrendering life
I see large buildings that cannot see strife
I see free salvation that is way under priced
I see a body called to poverty, by wealth be
enticed
And I know you see it too
Our allegiance has been spliced
Unsatisfied with the riches of the world
When God's kingdom should have sufficed

So I write to you
Who are soon to be
Revolutionaries
To encourage you in the cause
You will be influencing

I write to you to tell you that
You have all that you need
And that's not another book, facility
Conference or degree
It's not a bigger budget, membership
Network or building
For Christ conquered death with only a tree

And if you have more than that
How much more will He want to see
You see
You have all that you need
For you have
Breath, feet
Blood, tears
Pulse, hands
Eyes, ears
You have
Brothers, sisters
Resources, givers
A world full of sin
And a God that is bigger
You have all that you need and
You will need all that you have
For the life influenced by Christ
Cannot be given in halves
It will not spare a drop
It will not scare or stop
But will sell all it's got
To buy the treasure in the empty lot
You need all that you have
For you know the cost
It may cause you to toss away
Your money, your house
Your car, your clothes
The cause may cause you to lose all of those

But what if it costs your
Reputation
Position
Job and
Ambitions
Your
Identity
Decisions
Respect
Your best intentions?

You will need all you have
For you have all you need
And all you have is all He needs
For all you need is all He has

With great urgency I write this muse
For the one thing we do not have
Is an excuse

We have a mighty God who became poor and bruised
What we do not have is an excuse
We have the Holy Spirit inhabited for God's own use
What we do not have is an excuse
We have a sure resurrection, the power of death diffused
What we do not have is an excuse
We have the words of life, the greatest of news
What we do not have is an excuse

That is why I write to you this insisting issuance
And challenge you to lead with great prudence
To a world of darkness let us be a holy nuisance
As we lead the cause of Christ
Through the power of His influence

THE DAY DEATH DIES

I heard Death was on his bed
Nervous and sick from a bounty placed on his head

I heard Life was growing up
Strong and well fed
Ready to take over now that mortality was on its last leg

Life said, "I grew up watching Death
Resting in mischief, restless in rest
Robbing breaths from those who had so much left
He formed the fists with which men beat their breasts"

> "Cleft lips and HIV
> Starvation and diabetes
> Autism and mental disease
> Genocide and nationalities
> Typhoons and the raging seas
> Crusades concerning deities
> Suicide: self's fatality
> Murder and his justice's
> Subsequent penalty"

"I saw his blistered hands
Now rage stained and calloused red
I saw Death live," Life said

"But a day is coming, it is drawing nigh
A day when death will finally die"

"Many mis-think when thinking of me
Thoughts of a world where Death can no longer be
But after Death leaves
This won't just be a place where pain and disease
Are simply ceasing
But where all that is Death
Is replaced with
Life's beauty"

Life then recounted the countless products of his being

"The blind won't only see
    But will craft new colors
    Change the way we all perceive
    They will recreate our visual reality"

"The deaf won't only hear
    But will employ
        Grass blades and clouds
        Rivers and canals
    To compose one loud masterpiece
        For our ears
Oh, the deaf won't only hear"

"The poor won't only be made rich
    But the word itself will be stripped
        For all that was wealth

Will be reconsidered as hell
And all that was dearth
Will indeed inherit the earth"

"The prisoners won't only be released
But shall form the new police
And since there will be no crime
They shall spend their time
Arresting people in love
And writing citations for peace
Oh, the prisoners won't only be released"

He continued attenuating Death's time

"The dead won't only be made alive
But will redefine living
In the Kingdom of Life"

"Tears won't just stop falling from our eyes
But will flow ever heavily
From the joy inside"

"In the Kingdom of Life
The lame will run as horses
The widows made holy wives
The homeless will have so many houses
That they'll invite the formerly rich
To come live inside
In the Kingdom of Life"

"In the Kingdom of Life
Bruises will be prized
Enemies will be brides
Bullets will be revised
Melted down with guns and knives
To build bridges of unity
Across continental divides"

"In the Kingdom of Life
Wars won't only cease
But the standing armies
Of every tribe
Will be deployed as gardeners
To replant Eden in our own time"

"Seconds will be as heart beats
Minutes as breaths
Hours will be as moments and
Days, not as something
To be counted
But to be experienced"

"In the Kingdom of Life
Governments won't only be brought to their knees
But God Himself will join us
His people
Our king"

"In the Kingdom of Life
	Wrongs will no longer be right
	Darkness will be squandered by light
	The grave will be blotted out from our sight
	And justice will be allotted
	By God's unquestionable might"

Bear witness to the coming
	Of the Kingdom of Life
The beginning of truth
	The ending of strife
May we succeed from mortality
	To be eternity's allies
And speed along the day
	The day when Death dies

I BELIEVE IN JESUS

I believe in Jesus; the firstborn of all creation
The prelude to Adam, the author of Eden
By all, in all, through all, Genesis' reason
The husband of a new born bride
I believe Earth is His love's ultimate beacon

I believe in Jesus; the infant king
Ruler of the heavens, the universe's spring
Yet He took the frailest of forms
The weakest of things
For our mighty God was not too proud
For the stable and trough of Bethlehem's sting

I believe in Jesus; the forgiver of men
Since man would not come to God
God came to them
Though we spit in His face
Through our arrogance and sin
Holiness became flesh and said it was forgiven

I believe in Jesus; the perfection of the law
For creation was doomed
By the requirements it scrawled
But He came not to abolish correction
But fulfill us where we fall
And wrote a new law on our hearts
Love God and love all

I believe in Jesus; the Lord without a throne
He dumbfounded the masses
By not making the crown His own
Lost scores of followers by
Letting weakness be shown
And traded the palace for not having a home

I believe in Jesus; the tenant of the poor
He saw a beloved sister
Where the world saw a whore
He ate with those who
Weren't allowed through the temple's door
And taught us to live with less
So those with none could have some more

I believe in Jesus; the horribly betrayed
Unknown by the world He Himself had made
Handed over to death by a follower
To whom silver was paid
Disowned by a friend three times in one day

I believe in Jesus; the ever-turning cheek
No sword in His hand
He took the way of the weak
Redefined strength as beaten and meek
When men struck Him on His back
Only forgiveness did He speak

I believe in Jesus; the servant on the cross
To save the lives of the sinful
He considered His own life lost
Endured the torture of man
Whips and nails in His flesh were embossed
Received the wrath of God
Father punishing Son, the ultimate cost

I believe in Jesus; the flesh in the tomb
He bore the end of a normal human
As He was born of a human's womb
He died a criminal's death
And was buried in another man's room
God the Son lay dead, the lifeless groom

But I still believe in Jesus;
And the body of His resurrection
For He redefined life in death's final rejection
Showed holes in hands
To over 500 of His own selection
So that humanity would not
Be able to raise an objection
That Jesus Christ is God the Son
And has made the ultimate connection

I believe in Jesus;
And the responsibility of His ascension
He ascended to God's right hand
Forever in intersession
Leaving His truth in the hands of a few

The first to be called His Christians
His hands and feet are now the church
His timeless narrative expression

This is our heritage
They are our relatives
And this is our confession
We believe in Jesus the Christ
His
Death
Burial and
Resurrection

I BELIEVE IN SATAN

Her beauty hangs above me,
whispering angelically.
She leads me to the desert, testing me,
guiding me cunningly.
She nudges directionally,
sowing her seed in me.
I yield to her
    constantly,
    calmingly,
    relentlessly,
    religiously.
My Angel of Light,
my favorite Advisory.
My masqueraded Servant of Right,
my own worst Adversary.

She is known to many
and many know her
by her many signatures.
You may know her as

    Serpent,
    Accuser,
    Resident of Judas,
    Lucifer, Liar,
    Enticer,
    Ensnarer,
    Original Sinner,

Prowling Devourer,
Murderer, Tempter,
Satan, Schemer
Flaming Archer,
Roaring Leader,
Devil, Diablo,
Demone, Diable,
Teufel, Diavol,
Duivel, Diabolos.

She is many things to many people,
but the one thing she is to too few is
beautiful.

For
her most horrendous works are not her most
atrocious.
But her true acts of terror are
applauded by governments,
upheld by citizens,
enforced by armaments, and
accepted by Christians.
It's as if Satan has been christened;
her terror masked by her insistence that all is
well.
Her pitchfork pictation hides
her immanent identity,
for we are not so dull as to miss horns and a tail.
But we will call gluttony a luxury
and greedy consumerism a sale.

Lucifer's curves glisten on the racks;
her image priced for our fitting,
her pattern stitched for our dress.
She hoards up in accounts stacked with cash,
calls wealth God's bidding
and selfishness blessed.

The serpent whispers from the tree,
"You know good and evil,
for you have eaten of the fruit."
So we ignore loving our enemies
to fight them as war's new recruits.
Her favorite meal is poverty,
feasting on the poor by fattening the rich.

And my words now sound wrong,
for we have all been bewitched.
But don't let Satan's sexiest trick
make you believe God's will is your bliss.
For she knows that we all have this itch:
to find comfort for our greed and
justification for our selfishness.

We're made to believe
that Satan's for me,
that her presence is evil,
that if she speaks we will
hear her voice,

see her deception,
notice her noise,
end sin's inception.

But she is much slyer than our most cunning
detection,
for she has our most accepted activities
within her collection.
    Judging she calls correction.
    War is just protection.
    Justice is lethal injections.
    Changing our world is voting in elections.
    Questions are truth's rejection.
    Greed is God's blessed selection.
Satan does more than make sly suggestions.
She uses our best intentions as a means of
oppression.

So no,
I don't believe in Satan:
    the scapegoat for sin,
    the devil in his den,
    the shoulder speaking angle
    to the shoulder sitting angel.
But I do believe in an Adversary:
    the Advisor of the World,
    the Beauty found in hell,
    where death and fruit are curled.
I do believe in her -
    the Enemy of the Kingdom.

She's the shops where children sweat,
    the making of a victim.
She's the splitting of an atom,
    the stomach's empty growl.
She's the extortion of governance,
    the king's power gone foul.
She's the razor of depression,
    the severance of man from wife.
She's the disease of certain death,
    the corruption of given life.
She's the slums of Kenya,
    the mansions of L.A.,
and she's the one that tells us
    all of this is OK.

And that is her trick -
    to turn our world to hell,
to make you ignore what's sick
    by making you feel so well.

So yes,
we do have an Adversary
    whose reality we constantly shun.
And may we not be lured by her beauty,
    nor by her enchantment be won.

I BELIEVE IN THE SCRIPTURES

In the beginning there were words
    For no sky nor dirt
    Rocks nor birds
    Heaven nor Earth
    Death nor birth
Had yet been given proper syllabification
So nothing physical had yet entered creation
But despite the lacking of material manifestation
There did hang one true annunciation

Words
Words of God
Spoken Script
Speaking Scripture
Holy Writ
The Writing Builder
Building mountains out of nouns
        Plants and herbs from active verbs
        Planting nations in punctuation
        Preparing solar positions with prepositions
        Nature's narrative was rich with adjectives
But man was dirt and needed an additive
So God added His imperative
Impairing the dirt of its ability to be sedative
So came the breath of life
The words that made dirt our relative

We are born of Bible
Letters formed our limbs
How can I deny God's words
When they are written on my skin?
In this breath of life
God breathed to begin
An exhalation for the ages
The inspiration of men

You know the words of which I speak
You've memorized them

They are the
    Pentateuch
    Torah
    History Books
    Poets
    Major and Minor
    Prophets
    Synoptic Gospels
    Acts of the Apostles
    And their Epistles
They are our Scriptures
Those ancient divine whispers
Scribed by enlightened scripters
Passed down to modern listeners

The mouth by which the universe was founded
Is the fount on which our Scriptures are grounded
Listen to where the Bible was originally sounded

For it's far better than
What we have lobbied
Or from traditions copied
Or our own doctrines embodied
That Scripture says that Scripture is
        God breathed

That means
The breath that filled the nostrils of the ground
The life blown into dirt
The exhaling heartbeat that made the simple
renowned
That is what can be found
In what has been written down

So, I believe in the Scriptures
        Where God has breathed the breath of life
        Where we find the vows between
        Eternal husband and earthly wife
        Where saints and martyrs
        Find comfort for their strife
        And stone hearts come to get cut with a knife

I believe in the Scriptures
        When God breathed on dirt He got man
        When He breathed on man He got words
        The words are not in the dirt, but in the breath
        The breath passes from man to man
        Until they return to dirt
        The eternal chain of command
        The passing of words

And now the words are in our hands

But so often they're only found
Behind our lips or on our eyes
Within church doors in red and black lines
Printed on shirts, our commitment's disguise
What we claim as truth our lives say is a lie

But I believe in the Scriptures
    For those scribal scribbilings refuse
    To stay on the page
    For they give life so life is required to be paid
    The words in your Bibles
    Are not meant on paper to lay
    But to be resurrected in your flesh
    As you die to them everyday

I believe in the Scriptures
    For by them, through them
    And to them I was made
    They are the words that formed my bones
    And the ones that will call me from the grave
    They are the ink on my flesh
        the pen on my tongue
    They are the words by which creation begun
    And through which recreation will be done
They are the words of God and we are His listeners
        I believe God stills speaks
        I believe in the Scriptures

I BELIEVE IN GOD'S PEOPLE

Ours is a heritage of
Bloody stones and empty hands
Open homes and donated lands
A movement so bold its name
Book and practice were banned
Our brothers and sisters burned at the stake
The martyr's pulpit stand

Ours is a heritage of
Treating others as equals
Standing strong by being feeble
Surrendering wants to help those who are needful
Selling possessions to fit through the eye of the
needle
Giving up violence for the way of the peaceful

Ours is a heritage of God's people

It's a heritage of salty stories
It's the stigmata and poverty of Francis of Assisi
The small things with great love of
Theresa's leper colony
The substitutionary sacrifice at Auschwitz by
Maximillian Kolbe
The desert prayers of Antony
Clare's first female community
Bernard's massive move to the monastery
The 95 theses of Martin Luther

The non-violent fight for equality of
Martin Luther King Jr.
The unwritten names of history
Who died at the hands of rulers
The champions of Christianity
God's kingdom movers

This is our heritage
The lives and deaths of God's people
They are our predecessors in the Book of Life and
I believe we are writing the sequel

I believe in this people
We hold the pens
The world has the page
Our heart is the ink and
The words our hands engage
Let us write a love story, my people
Full of smiles, kisses, and blood
Let our novel be as rich
As the tales from which we have come

I believe in this people
We will be the mustard seed
Small in posture, rich in potency
Let the world crush us
Up we will spring
For no stomp is too severe

No foot is too heavy
To keep us from rising up
To claim the cross's victory

I believe in this people
Not because we have done anything
Worthy of believing
But for the very fact that we are nothing
We are a broken people
Comprised of broken persons
A sinful race
Filled with sinful notions
A body of hypocrisy
Contradicting ourselves with every motion

But that is why I believe in this people
Because it's not who we are but whose we are
That makes us believable

We are not born of man like all the nations of this world
But are the children of God
The Almighty's boys and girls

I believe in God's people
For He makes us do crazy things
Moses left a palace to free his people from slavery
Joshua walked around Jericho for a week
David took on a giant with tiny stones and a sling
Job refused to blame God though he lost everything
Hosea married a prostitute

To show God's love symbolically
Mary believed she was pregnant
Though she'd never been with a man intimately
Joseph had faith that his soon to be wife
Had not been cheating
John the Baptist ate insects and dunked people in the
Jordan claiming something great was coming
Peter gave up his job, possessions, and
Home to follow a passing missionary
And a poor Jewish Nazarene
Gave up His life willfully
Though He was guilty of nothing
Now apostles, disciples, believers, and Christians
Have for 2,000 years changed everything
Because they believe that this Jesus' love
Is more powerful than anything

That is why I believe in the people of God
For our strength is not in what we have
But what we have given up
Our power is not our own
But in the one who bore the cross
We need not worry about what we gain
For we win when we have lost
We are not perfect
But realize that grace will pay our cost

I believe in this people
Because I believe in their God

RESURRECTING CRUCIFIXION

My conversion was coercion
Coerced by convicting conversations
To converge my words with the sinner's recitation
To diverge my works towards redemption
To submerge myself in baptism
I converted to this religion
And became covert in my Sunday operation
As I went undercover for fear of condemnation

They never really asked me to die
Just handed me salvation

They never really asked for my heart
But gave me a Sunday sensation

They never really asked for my mind
But wanted contemplation

They never really asked for my tongue
But wanted my proclamation

They never really asked for my finances
But wanted a small donation

They never really asked me to be the church
Just had me come to a location

They never really asked me to be transformed
Just put my sin on probation

I seemed to have passed over crucifixion
To attain resurrection

I was never subjected
My life never arrested
Never laid my sin on its death bed
Only had to answer a few simple questions

I said the prayer but my life never gave proof
It's like I ignored the dare
By simply acknowledging the truth

And

Many of you were like me
Passed over cross and grave
For a stake in heaven

Go to church
But are still in search
Of that real salvation

Maybe it's because
We feared damnation
Or were told we could have life
Without tasting degradation

But taking up a cross
Wasn't a suggestion
It was an invitation

We claim rebirth
without dying first

That's like

Dating without fidelity
Marriage without monogamy
Fertilization without intimacy
A child without pregnancy
Labor without laboring

We want to be raised up before we start laying
    Down our life
    To be the wife
    Of the husband
    Who loved us
    Despite our sin's cruel might

We are trying to experience the morning
Without ever tasting the night
But how can you know darkness
If you have never seen the light

It is time for us to die

Time to die
To our conceptualized God
The one who allows us to buy
But never be bought
The one who allows us to prosper
But never consider the cost
The one who allows us to catch others
Without ever being caught
The one who allows us to ask everyone else to do
What we will not
The one who allows our lives to be wrong
As long as we have the right thoughts
The one who doesn't teach us to love
But teaches us to do what we ought

The Son of God came and died
For our sins to redeem
And when He took up the bread and took up the cup
He said, "Do this in remembrance of Me"
So when He took up His cross
And told us that He wants
Us to take up ours accordingly
He did not mean this purely symbolically
Or simply literally
But He bids us come, be strapped to the cross
And die to the life we were leading

So if we have been crucified with
Christ can we go on living?
By no means!

If you want to been raised you must take up your tree
And that's not salvation by works
But the effect of causality
For it's not I who lives
But Christ who lives in me
And the life I live in the body
I live by the faith He is providing

But that's not the way we're living

We don't want to be broken
    But we want His bread
We don't want to surrender our own
    But we want His flesh
We don't want to be pierced
    But we want His open side
We don't want to be poured out
    But we want His wine
We don't want Judas
    But we want his silver pay
We don't want Pilate
    But we want the pearly gates
We don't want thorns
    But we do want a crown
We don't want to be stripped naked
    But we do want a gown
We don't want Gethsemane
    But we watch Him cry
We don't want Golgotha
    But we need Him to die

We don’t want the cross
    But we yearn for redemption
We don’t want crucifixion
    But we crave resurrection
If you want His life you must come to die
    You may just want His love
        But He longs for you to be His bride

THE KNEE, THE CHAPEL, THE SUIT, AND THE RING

I am a fugitive of the law
The outlaw of Gethsemane
The light of the world
Yet darkness overtakes Me
Let this cup pass, don't let them take Me
For this flesh is real, these lungs inhaling
And My nerves aren't impervious
To wood, nails, and hammering
My spirit is willing
But this flesh is so weak
The inside is spilling but
What holds it is bleak
Like this cup that sits before Me
I can't lift to drink
Why must the chalice be so sour
For the wine to be so sweet?
Why must I be enslaved to torture
For her to be free?
Yet not as I will
But let Your will be
For I can't make her mine
Without proposing
And I can't propose
Without taking a knee

For you I kneel
For you I'll die
Your will be done
Just accept My bride

I am a culprit on trial
I created the universe
The filer of the firmament
The stylist of violet
The complier of Pilate
I abdicated sin and lived perfect
Yet to these produced powers
I fall under judgment
I look out and see My beloved
Those of My Father's covenant
Those for whom I was made incarnate
Standing in this square of government
Yelling "Crucify Him!" to their governor
I came to be their comforter
By becoming their prisoner
Yet they call me a swindler
The orthodox pillager
A slandering sinister
The libel listener
As I heard crucifixion become the crowd's signature
I saw a chapel start to form around the perimeter
Soon every person in attendance became a
contributor
To the marriage service being administered
For we can't be wed without a minister
So may Pilate give Me away

And it can't be binding without witnesses
But what a crowd we've gathered today
For you I'm judged
For you I'll die
Disowned by My people
To accept My bride

I am a convict on death row
Marching to execution
My tool of death they place on My back
Like an inmate forced to wire his chair for
electrocution
Sinful no, but guilty yes
Guilty of creating revolution
Not one of violence or death
But one that challenged
Religious, political, and social institutions
For pursuing righteousness I fell under persecution
The Creator condemned to crucifixion
By a created prosecution
They sentenced Me to restitution
By handing Me the world's solution
Making Me the substitution
For the punishment of pollution
Taking Me through
Dusty streets
To prove My Father's
Not a god of retribution
But one of justice and resolution
So I march across this created rock
With cross embossed as He had planned

For I can't take your hand
Unless I walk down the aisle
And I can't take the stand
Unless dressed in wedding style
So may these streets be the way
And let these beams be My suit and tie
As I walk to you on our wedding day
The nails, the hammer, the crucified
For you I march
For you I'll die
I take up My cross
To accept My bride

I am a criminal on the cross
Don't even get My own hill for this sentence
But have to share it with ordinary thieves
For an ordinary thing is this instance
We hang, they wait
We writhe, they play
Casting wages for My garment
Making payments as I make their payment
Not just theirs but My disciples
Who despise this arrangement
Those to whom I hang for entertainment
And those to whom My hanging is their estrangement
I live and die for their containment in My home
For grace's attainment in My fold
For I have proposed
And I have kneeled
I have disclosed
The location of our nuptial deal

I have composed
Myself with this cross suit and zeal
Now I have transposed
Iron stakes into our wedding seal
For we cannot be wed without a band
So these spikes will be our rings
You'll slip mine first into these hands
But you'll have to wait three days
Until yours I bring
For you the nails
For you I'm crucified
For you I'm forsaken
An acceptable bride

THE SOUND OF GRACE

Before tanned skin was ever stretched
Over eardrums
Before sound's mallets ever caressed
Our inner tympanum
Before man started speaking
With the chatter of his tongue
There was the sound of none
Then silence was put in a conundrum
The stillness of void
Pierced by
The creation of noise
The booming of words
The beginning of Earth

New birth could be heard
As life began to spurt
Plants stretched and yawned from their seeds
Water went rushing through gills in the seas
Cries from the newborns of nature's pregnancy
And lies were overheard behind the fruit of a tree
Hear the sounds of deceit
The bite of an apple
The hiss from the mud
The exit in shackles
The crying of blood
The snake's cruel rattle

The roaring of floods
The hammers of Babel
The fruit as it buds

Listen to the mountain of man
Shift and scrape away from Mt. Zion
The mountain of God

Hear the echo of our cries
As they fall, not rise
In the canyon between
Us and the Creator of our life

We are destined to die
Our sin has earned this penalty

Can't you hear our flesh crinkle with age
Withering with disease?
Listen to these cancers grow
Taking life out of our families
The final word of infirmaries

Harken to the weapons of war
The slaughtering of our sons
The making of enemies
Hear the dropping of bombs
The trampling of beauty

Take in the sound of our dying
The cries of poverty
The crush of pornography

The lies of adultery
The lust of idolatry
We are lost in the noise of our own depravity

Can't you perceive the bellowing laugh of the grave
The sharp pitch of death and his sting?
The tomb's mouth is wide
Its belly is hungry

Listen to the rebellion of man
The haughty scoffs of his pride
Hear the heart of God break
As we defile His design

Amazing space
How deep the ground
That separates humanity
We all are lost
And now we've found
The blinding sound of our fatality

But God's grace would not give up His bride to be
Our sin's disease brought forth
The Son of Deity

Listen to
The hushed talk of Pharisees
The betrayal begins
The clanging of silver
The exchanging of bribes
The passing of bread

The drinking of wine
The tears of Gethsemane
The garden's cries
The presence of soldiers
The kiss full of lies
The sentence of Pilate
The crowd's voices rise
The crack of the whip
The cat with tails of nine
The piercing of nails
The hammer, it drives
The groan of the cross
The Savior, He dies

For our sin He came
For our sin He died
With our sin we slayed His
Sinless life

Now in the ground He lies
After paying our price
For we could not make right
The sound of our strife

But there are whispers from the grave
Shuffles in the dark
As dead eyes awake
Death's end gets its start

Hear the trampling of skin
The sound of grace coming to life
Hear the last breaths of sin
The husband rises for His wife

Amazing faith
How deep the vow
That engaged a wretch like me
All was lost
To make us found
The death of heaven's mystery

Listen to the stone cower from the mouth of the grave
Hear the wrappings rip from the body that is raised
Can't you hear the resounding brilliance
Of He who had died?
Listen to the proclamation, "He is not dead! He is alive!"

Now all that was dark may be brought to the light
Now all that was dead may be given new life
Now all that was wrong may be made right
Now all that was sinful may be forgiven in God's sight

Hear the sweet sound of shame
Running from your heart
Hear your old songs of pain
Turn into "How Great Thou Art"
Hear your pity turn to praise

Hear your passion find its place
Hear your beating heart skip
As you hear God call your name

You are not alone
Heaven ripped open and forgave you
You are not meant to die
But God did in your place just to save you
You are not an accident
He created creation to create you
And you are not forgotten
Just remember those horns will blow
When He returns to reclaim you

Amazing grace
How sweet the sound
That saved humanity
We once were deaf
But now we hear
The shouts of His victory

CHEW (meditation)

"Repent for the kingdom of heaven is near"
"Repent for the kingdom of heaven is near"
"Repent for the kingdom of heaven is near"
"Repent for the kingdom of heaven is near"

You can almost hear
The crackling of vowels
The crunch of consonants
As my tongue and lips
Play catch with
The same eight words
Like they're in conversation with
Themselves

"Repent for the kingdom of heaven is near"
The words start asking questions like:
How do I repent for my transgressions?
What is this kingdom that moves in
Without a procession?
Is there a difference between earthly empires
And one from heaven?
How close is "near" and what is its expression?

If Spirit is stomach
And food required digestion
Then it is the process of chewing
That we may call meditation

It's the required repetition
Of holy recollection
Re-collecting words
In murmuring bites of reflection
But we prefer ingestion instead of obsession

We would rather fill our bellies with a
Fast food Sunday of
Spoon-fed liquid lunch
Than to sit with eight words
And let that be enough

So to a generation
That requires meditation
But has forgotten how to
I tell you one thing

Don't forget to chew

For you have eaten much
Shoved God in your mouth
Plunged mysteries down your throat
Filled your bellies with life
And transformed transformation into waste

You have been served
Ancient delicacies of
Grace and truth

But wash them down with
A communion cracker
And a shot of juice

Don't forget to chew
For you have tasted nothing
And digested even less
You have mouthfuls of church
But I can't even smell Christ on your breath
Chew a little longer on the Bread of Life
Those loaves of truth will age in your mouth
Like the finest of wines

Keep a word between your teeth at all time
Like "love"
Oh, never stop biting on love!
Let it get stuck between your molar and wisdom
Suck on it until all the flavor has gone
And you've tasted all the subtleties of
    Peace
    Joy
    Sacrifice
    Suffering
    Passion
    Intimacy and
    Hope
Found in that one sweet bite of love

Then, once every taste is divined
Swallow and let the truth you've refined
Permeate your life
Medicate your strife
Renovate your mind
Penetrate what's blind

Meditate a little longer on the Bread of Life
Prepared for you
Eat all you can of these loaves of truth
But remember this, my hungry family
Never forget to chew

THE NUMBER (prayer)

How many times have you prayed in your life?
Now I'm not asking
How many lists you've made
    Or
How many religious instructions you've obeyed
    Or
How many games of "Guilty Christian" you've played
    Or
How many public speeches you've relayed
    Or
How many recitations you've portrayed

I'm asking
How many times have you prayed?

How many times have you
Cried, whimpered
Sighed, whispered
Tried to listen
Died and risen?

How many times have you approached God honestly?
Asked for nothing, but got everything?
Had everything to hide, but hid nothing?
Said not a word, but spoke endlessly?
Never opened your eyes, but saw eternity?

How many times
Have you reached inside
Yourself so deeply
That you pulled out something you didn't recognize?
How many times have you approached your Maker
Not as who you want to be
Not as who you wish you were
Not as who you think you are
Not as who you ought to be
But just as you are
With all the dirt
That covered you
When God first fell in love with you?

How many times have you run to your
Lover for passion, your
Provider for rations, your
Father for lessons, your
Instructor for lashings?

Oh, how many times have you prayed?

For your God's ear, it waits
For one drop of confession
One honest expression
One wild connection

Don't approach the living God with dead prayers
But come to Him when your lifeless prayers are dead
And the Spirit on your tongue is dripping with life

Then every syllable you speak will be a divine trade
Your mouth will leak
With the flood of praise you've made
Then the number you seek
Will be far too high to be weighed
And you'll never be able to answer the question
"How many times have you prayed?"

ISAIAH 58 (fasting)

Appetite is affixed onto my calendar
I've carved out times so I could be a carnivore
Three times a day I bow at my food's altar
To calm the growling inside I call hunger

My Islamic friends have a similar culture
Only instead of bowing to food
They stop everything to pray to their father
They even have names

Fajr
Dhuhr
Asr

But all I have is

Breakfast
Lunch
Dinner

I am accustomed to being a consumer
When my body weakens, I tremble
When my stomach hungers, it growls
When my tongue lusts, I drool
When my eyes desire, I feed

It never ceases to amaze me
That my body has this thrice-daily anomaly
That warns me when it gets hungry

But
Once
Just once
I want my spirit to grumble in my gut so loudly
That it forces my knees to bend and my arm
To wave down God like a waiter
And order the largest portion of revelation on the menu

I want to hunger for a different kind of food

I want to salivate over generous portions of grace
Lick my lips at the smell of wisdom
Develop a wicked sweet tooth for truth

I want my inmost being to growl for
    The wheat of the Father
    The meat of the Son
    The fruit of the Spirit
A three course meal
I want a different food pyramid

A steady diet of the divine
A fast from any food money can buy
Where I only eat what I can find
Within the cracks of the bread
And the pour of the wine

I want to go out to eat
The dark corners of town have all the best restaurants

And there's always an open seat
I want to prepare a table for God
On the streets and the gutters
Invite His choicest of guests
The orphans and widows
His weakest of lovers

I want to hunger with the hungry
Thirst with the thirsty
Be penitent with those in penitentiary
And infect myself with other's infirmaries

I want to binge on righteousness
And guzzle streams of peace
Until the world's belly is full of restoration
And redemption flows free

I want to prefer the flavor of words over food
Oh God, let me acquire a taste for You
Let bread loose its flavor
I long to taste my Savior
Come fast, my fast
Save me from my hunger
For the Spirit's noise in my stomach grows fierce
And I'm famished for my Lover

So I will break up with breakfast
I'll lunge away from lunch
I will deny myself of dinner
Until Your portion is enough

," SAYS THE WRITER (study)

A message from the apocryphal book of love
written on my mouth
to the eyes and minds of the bride of Christ
concerning what has been written down
"I'm waiting for you
        ," says the Writer

"I've spent the entirety of history
interacting with humanity
who've penned My biography
and I'd love to share it with you"

"I've sketched outlines of My face
in the pages of My book
        so you can see My wrinkles
        more smile lines from rejoicing looks
        than from a furrowed brow
I even penciled in bags under My eyes
        so you can see how
they formed from an eternity of watching
        My loved ones hour by hour"

"It's all there
        ," says the Writer

"You need only look a little longer at the
        genius of Genesis -
how I patched you into the genus of existence
        You exist because of Exodus

40 years I spent with your ancestors in the wilderness
Oh, study My writings
," says the Writer
"So you don't make the same mistakes they did"

"I've hidden Myself in Leviticus
Try to find Me
and I'll whisper secrets in your ear
once you do
I proved My desire in Jeremiah
Come meet Me inside the dried papyri
and I'll show you how I pursued My people
though they left Me when they
found some power to acquire"

Listen to the Writer

"I've painted My every feature
in the creases of this tome
Curl up with Me and see what I have shown:
tears from the flood
My correcting and guiding rod
wings that stretch up above
showing that I'm enough
See My face in these pages of love
I wrote history so you'd know My law
I wrote poetry so you'd feel My touch
I wrote prophecy so you'd hear My tongue
I wrote in the first century so you'd know I've come

And I wrote eternal truth in bright red
so you'd see the passion of My blood
Get to know me
," says the Writer
"for I formed the universe so I could get to know you
Study the curves of My form
as you learn the shapes of My words"

"Open My mouth;
I want to tell you intimate things
Loosen My lips;
let My white teeth pages move free
Don't still My tongue;
spend hours listening with your eyes as you read
Learn the tenor of My voice
so when I speak you'll know it's Me
," the Writer pleads

"I'm here to rescue you
From the lines of what it means to study
Don't come to the mouth of the Mighty One to
memorize
summarize
identify or
justify
Let me surprise you"

"It's not a place for
arguments
dogmatics

apologetics or
mathematics
Let me define you"

Spend time with the audible divine
contemplate
meditate
examinate
communicate

"Let Me inside you"

"I'm here
," says the Writer

"Within ancient ink there is a living God
Stare deeply as you read My eyes
and I'll whisper to you of outrageous love"

TWO COATS (simplicity)

Discipline me in simplicity
I've got two coats too many and walk one mile too short
Discipline me in simplicity
I've got silver-lined pockets and a sheath for my sword
Discipline me in simplicity
I've got more than plenty and a silo for the rest to store
Discipline me in simplicity
My heart breaks under the weight of all I have
But my eyes still lust for more
Oh Lord!
Discipline me in simplicity

For my people and I are simply a city
Implicitly drunk on the liquor of industry
We would rather buy a decorated sign
That says "Live Simply"
Than to simply live without all the trapping of clout
We're told we need by our TVs
Discipline me in simplicity

Redefine for me the definition of enough
For if it's less than I have and less than I want
Then what else can enough be
If not only my needs
Discipline me in simplicity

Teach me to sell, for I know only how to buy
Teach me how to apply the word simplify

Naked I came into this world
And naked will I die
And if my righteousness is filthy rags
Than what clothes are my crimes?
Just dress me in those righteous rags
And sell the contents of the closets I call mine
For my hangers are better dressed
Than my brothers and sisters living outside

Teach my to apply the word simplify
For my people and I long for this mystery

Discipline me in simplicity
Place me in the context of Your
Economic ecumenical community
Where I can't claim excess when others are lacking
For what right have I to wealth
When poverty is attacking my siblings?
Where my worth is not weighed by the gold in my hand
But by the crown worn by my King
Where banks are replaced by offering plates and
Two-person tables for neighborhood dining
Where we share everything in common
And hold nothing individually
Where the hungry feast because the fed are fasting
Where I learn to go without
So others no longer have to plead

Where there is enough for everyone's need
But not everyone's greed
Smaller portions
Fewer things
More of You
And less of me

My people and I are ready for Your victory
So discipline us, Lord
In the weakening power of Your simplicity

A CANDLELIGHT DINNER FOR TWO
(solitude)

One day
God slipped me a divine invitation
To a candlelight dinner for two

He drew a beautiful incantation
That made me feel less persuaded and more pursued
"Come out from the multitude," He wrote
"I want to dine with you in solitude"
Immediately I was in pursuit
Leaving the audience of eyes I was in service to
I had always been a victim of public servitude
    Needing people to see me
    Recognition was my being
    Attention gave me meaning
    If ever I went somewhere alone
    I left a little bird behind
    Singing of me, tweeting
But now I was retreating
    Away from the eyes of others
    Into a night alone with my Father
I followed my divine invitation farther and farther
Until I was no longer able to walk
And that's where I found the table
    At the line where the wilderness begins
    And civilization stops

There was God
    Dressed in stillness
    Robed in rest
The table set
    With the utensils of quietness

We began by feasting on
My insecurities
The appetizer appeased
My appetite for approval's applause
No longer did I hunger for other's
    Healing attention gauze
For I was whetted with undivided
Obsession from my God

I started to forget the multitude
As I dined with Him in solitude

Then the entrée
Made its way
To my plate
And as it took shape
I started to shake
For I saw on the tray
A clock that was sure to take
What was surely mine
For I realized
We would be
Eating time

But as I digested the time-tested clock
I stopped
Constantly checking my watch
And only watched His eyes on mine

The longer I spent away from the multitude
The more time was consumed in solitude

Once the main course was finished
And time was devoured
I got the urge to leave
And tell everyone of my divine encounter
But He told me it was not yet time
To depart from the desert
For he had prepared for me one final dessert
        Now that I had been taught
                To dine with God in a quiet place
                The eyes of others to forsake
                In His presence to make time wait
        Now I was ready for the softness of His voice
        The icing of His words
        In one sweet sentence of His cake

Finally I escaped from the voices of the multitude
And heard my God whisper softly to me in solitude

And that's where He's inviting you
God is slipping into your hands
A divine invitation to a
Candlelight dinner for two

An invitation to
Hide from the eyes that surround you
Rid yourself of the lies that hound you
Break free from this thing
Called time that enshrouds you
And to be alone with the one who is all around you

Hear His voice, for you are being pursued
"Come out from the multitude," He says
"I want to dine with you in solitude"

A HOLY GAME (submission)

"Let's play a holy game,"
    says the Christian in submission

"I'll serve you
    and you do the same
We'll play pattycake with the planet
    taking slaps from those who
    haven't yet learned how to play
Let's hold out our pink hands for free hits
    from our neighbors, enemies
    friends, and governments
I'll go first
    so you can follow the
    tempo of my claps
We'll put the world back in rhythm
    by taking the rap for that
    which we did not commit"

"Let's play a holy game,"
    says the Christian in submission

"I'll draw treasure maps to secret places
    and you'll find those who hate you most once
    you've finished walking all the paces
We'll open our chest together
    to show those who oppose us
    the richness of our treasure
Let's unroll all the maps we hold
    until all our enemies are forgiven

And if in the end we have nothing left
    we will have the riches of submission"

"Let's play a holy game of musical chairs
    where we follow the laws our kings declare
    but still end up in their prisons
For we're dancing along, but to a different song
    the wild dance of humble submission"

"Let's play a holy game of make believe
    I'll dress up like Jesus
    and you can look like me
We'll pretend that everyone is our Lord
    and give them whatever their mouths do plead
Let's use our mother's makeup to
    make everyone look like a queen
We'll adorn those who despise us
    and beautify our enemies
For in this game we gave them
    God's authority"

"Let's play a holy game, my friend,"
    says the Christian in submission

"For my former opponents are sore losers
    and I long to see them to win
So we'll write new rules on both our cheeks
    so when the winners slap their victory beats
    they'll have freshly printed ink
    on both their hands
        their very own submission plans"

"Let's play a holy game of hide and seek
    where God is constantly hidden in everyone
    and you and I always peek
    into their closets to see God chuckling
    behind their hangers of clothes
We'll tag them and say, 'You're it!'
    'I Am,' they'll now know
And we'll chase each other
    down halls and into
    new laughing wardrobes"

"Let's submit to the picture of the Spirit
    in all God made
Let's play a holy game"

"We'll join the winning team
They're the ones with the lowest score
    and blood covering their jerseys
No need to worry
    the blood comes not from those we are opposing
For we lose until the game is won
    and that's the only game known as holy"

"Let's play the game of submission,"
    must say every Christian

For the game of the cross
    considers all loss
    for the sake of everyone Christ is in

So we submit to them:
    husbands to their wives
    wives to their husbands
    citizens to their governments
    and the rod of their punishments
    children to their parents
    and parents to instruction
    Christians to their enemies
    even to destruction

It's a game of sacrifice
    a game of true freedom
Let's play a holy game
    the game called submission

YOUR BODY, THE CHURCH (service)

Your body is housing a church service

And the whole neighborhood is invited

The worship times are posted on every breath
And each person who steps in sight is
Given an invitation to join every limb
Of your body's congregation

Your body is housing a church service

Your steeple hand will raise in answer
To the questions of the mourning Earth
You keep your steeple hand high
For you know the reason why
The mourning ones search

Your body is housing a church service

The cathedral doors of your mouth
Are pried ever open
Letting the organ's gospel music
Dancing on your tongue
Spill out like an ancient Galilean song
"Repent for the kingdom of heaven is near"
And it is
Just look at you

Your body is housing a church service

Your church bell eyes chime
Swinging east and west
Perceiving every cry
Serving every request
The whole block responds to your brassy sets
Bringing their sick, lost, and lame
To sit on the love of your steps

Your body is housing a church service

Your heart's a parsonage
With countless rooms and unparalleled hospitality
Burdened travelers and broken souls
Find a home within the room service of your heart
Ever occupied, but there's always a vacancy

Your body is housing a church service

Your thighs will serve as ornate pews
A lap for the weary
A leg up for those who lose

Your fingers are preachers
As they dry the tears of broken hearts
And scrub the dirt off homeless sneakers
Oh how the world loves the words of your fingers

Your every exhale is a hot meal
    Alluring the hungry into God's kitchen

Your every step onward
    Toward a brother
Downward to a sister
    Plucks the tune of "He Paid it All"
Your legs are the altar call

Your every word is worship
    Drawing the choir
Into the eternal song

Your body is housing a church service

But it's unlike any you've ever seen
    For it is not held behind
Wood doors and orthodoxy
    But is built inside your very form
And exists not for services but to house servicing

Your body is a church
    Your body is a service
Your body is housing a cross-load of work
    For it's in serving that you worship
You see

Your body is housing a church service

The whole neighborhood is in attendance
    And the Friend is sitting on the front row
Singing His heart out in rejoicing observance
    To every move of your body's wild service

I HAVE A CONFESSION TO MAKE
(confession)

I have a confession to make:
Grace is more racy than homosexuality
More full of life than teenage pregnancy
More captivating than pornography
Grace is far more potent than anything
That could make us guilty
But we treat grace like a child
When we hide our sin and question its ability

I have a confession to make:
The true measure of a Christian
Is not how well their sin is hidden
Or how many church services they have attended
Or how low the number of transgressions
They have committed is
The true measure of a Christian
Is hidden in Christ
Whom they have been given

I have a confession to make:
There is now no condemnation
For those who are in Christ Jesus
And that goes for
The gossip as well as the alcoholic
The greedy as well as those in adultery
The apathetic as well as the addict
The judgmental as well as the homosexual

We're all looking for something we can throw
At anyone whose sin looks worse than our own
But we are all sinners; we've all been exposed
So none of us are left with even a single stone

I have a confession to make:
Anyone who calls themselves a Christian
Makes the ultimate confession
For Christ did not come for the healthy
But for those in need of medication
The prostitutes, murderers, and those in rehabilitation
So if you claim to be a Christian
You claim to be in need of powerful salvation

I have a confession to make:
We are all trapped in shame
Until we give sin a name
For we all play this game
Where we try to look the same
By modifying and hiding our behavior
So no one can see our sin and make us a stranger
But what we don't realize is that we are in danger
For if we act like we have no sin
We live like we need no savior

I have a confession to make:
My eyes, lips, and mind are stained and unclean
From images, drinks, and words
That would have condemned me
But I'm not saved because I'm perfect
Or have my sin under control
I'm saved because I need saving and that is the Gospel

I have a confession to make:
You no longer have to hide
For God has seen everything that you are
And still came for you and died
It doesn't matter if everyone rejects you
You are still His spotless bride

So come
Make your confession
And rob sin of its power
For what strength does it have
If shame has been devoured?

Come make your confession
And make room for healing
Both for yourself and for others
Whom with your very sin they have been dealing

Come make your confession
And rid the church of its judges
For if everyone is confessing
There's no room to make judgments

I have a confession to make:
God is not condemning His own
And we should not be trying
To play His role
So let us start to pick up our crosses instead of our stones
Hurl rocks of Gospel at each other instead of blows
Open our mouths to confess and forgive
Instead of keeping them closed
And overlook the speck in another's eye
To attend to the plank in our own

I have a confession to make
And church, it's time you made yours too
For Christ did not die so that we may hide
But to love us in spite of the wrong that we do

So come
Speak your sins
On the altar of confession
It doesn't matter if the world says you're condemned
For all God will speak is salvation

THE ANIMAL ON YOUR TONGUE
(worship)

In these last few days
God has grown tired of being admired
By the worship of those who
Come to Him because it's required

In these last few days
He's decided to
Retire the altar fire and animal burn-up
For a much higher means of tangible worship

In these last few days
God has decided to pour Himself into a goblet
And let it
Get tipped
Over
To pour into the bones of those
He's chosen to worship

In these last few days
God has poured out His Spirit

Now this
Divine Wine
This Liquid God
Intoxicates His remnant
With His different characteristics
His spiritual gifts

To one God manifests Himself
As He did with the prophets
They dream dreams and see things
The way God intended it
To another God is uncovered
As a wise and patient brother
They don't teach like the others
But speak heaven's mind instead
For they have fragments of God
Lodged inside their heads
To yet another God is revealed
With hands that cannot help but heal
They wrap arms around the dying
And lay palms on the ill

The flood of God drenches the world's face
With gifts of
Knowledge
Discernment
Power and
Faith

So let us make ready our
Gifts for that day
That day we come together
To worship the one in whose Spirit we bathe

Make ready for worship
Those who have received what the heavens gave

Let the prophets gather their visions
May the wise ones prepare their lessons
Let the faithful drag along mountains
May the discerning ready their questions
Let the psalmists make their revisions
May the elders wage their decisions
And let this Spirit that is in all of us
Empower the body to bridge all divisions

Make ready for worship
For you cannot show up empty handed
For you have been filled with the one true God
And it is for praise that He landed
On you

We're used to
    Coming to the Sunday show
    Sitting quietly on our favorite row
    Singing songs we already know
    Sipping grapes and eating dough
    Soaking in words, going with the flow
But in these last few days
God has decided to throw
Himself into the midst of all that's below

So no

You can no longer just show up
And expect to worship
You must make ready your cup

To present to the one
Who's filled you with love

In these last few days
Worship has changed
For everyone brings
A piece of their King
And we piece Him together as our voices join to sing
    One brings a song
        Another a sermon with potency
    A brother brings a prayer
        A sister brings some poetry
    Everyone brings their share
        And shares it all; nobody
    Comes without their gift
        But brings their all openly

We worship because
We have been totally filled
In presenting our gifts
It's the church that we build
We sing, not in routines
But because we are utterly thrilled
For it is upon us
God's Spirit has completely spilled

So I say to everyone whom God's Spirit has entered
You can't just show up to worship
But must
Bring your gifts to praise the Giver

So prepare for the slaughter the animal on your tongue
To be poured out on the altar within the ear of our God

PAPER HIGHWAY (guidance)

And there was
stretched out
before me
a paper thin highway
straight as a pencil
only my lead feet hadn't
yet learned to write
As my head hung in spite
I saw small instructions
repeating the words
"Left, right
Left, right"

My feet started to trace
the paper highway's phrase

As I quickened my pace
more complicated sayings started
conjugating on the pavement -
quotations like "Press on to the goal"
and, "Take hold
of that which has taken hold
of you"

It was then I drew
my vision
away from the cement
only to find a person
tap dancing writings and
jogging out inscriptions

This was no abandoned road
but a highway for travelers
centuries old

Once again
I quickened
the pace of my feet's scribbling trace
to try and catch this wise word
inventor
for it hadn't taken long
but he had become
my long-stretch-highway
mentor

But the faster I skipped
the more words I missed
so I turned back to clean up
my footstep slips

And as sure as I did
there was down the road
someone standing where I was
not a few strides ago

Lead feet
head in spite
he started tracing my steps
"Left, right
Left, right"
It was then that I realized
this road is not for me;
this narrow path
commutes and communicates
to a whole family

My steps became
deliberate
meticulous
even independent
for I wanted this new
pavement student
to catch every lesson
on the highway's
syllabus

So I stopped for just a moment
and smiled as I inscribed
this omen:

"You've found yourself here
on the thin highway to God
An eternity of feet have gone before you
etching wisdom in lead and in blood

There are lifetimes to learn
  so walk patiently and occasionally in silence
Don't pass over any word
  without taking in its guidance
For everyone needs a mentor
  someone to go before them
For our God's a wild runner
  and we must be trained to endure Him
But you are not alone
  and I can't help but remind you
To step passionately on this road of life
  for there is always someone else following
    behind you"

HOW CAN WE BUT CELEBRATE
(celebration)

Someone should sound heaven's alarm for
There is no one watching the front gate
For every eye of
God
Angel
Cherubim and
Saint
Is fixed on this ancient synagogue
Where we now congregate

How can we but celebrate?

For where two or more are gathered
In the name of the Father
There is erected a holy alter
Tall tower
Temple
All-powerful
Symbol
Where there is a tango or two step
Waltz or mosh pit
Any form of the divine dance and
The one who invented legs
Is in attendance
How can we but jive when
The Creator-Savior is in this common place

How can we but celebrate?

The Almighty is performing
On the dead things of the earth
An autopsy
Resurrecting and reassembling
For Himself a globe-sized body

For there are
        Fingers in Argentina
            Thighs in Thailand
                Feet in the Northeast
                    Legs in the Midwest
And in this very temple
A gorgeous bride
Is being assembled as
        Shoulders
            Shins and
                Knuckles
Worship in our midst today

How can this body but celebrate?

Look around you
God is pregnant with recreation
And is going into labor
For in these chambers
        Strangers are made neighbors
            Enemies made brothers
                Sinners made sisters

The word family is getting bigger
As we are recreated

How can we but celebrate it?

Watch the Lord's table
For Welch's and saltines
Are becoming forearms and arteries
How can mouths but drop in astonishment
As God Himself
Crawls inside of us
As we feast on the mystery
Of the cross's plate

How can bellies and mouths but celebrate?

Heaven is shouting inside
Every member of every member
Just look behind the smile
Of their pearly gates
And you'll see God singing
At the top of His lungs

How can we but celebrate?

The ear that knows every note
And foreseen every song
Has bent down through
Atmosphere and roof
To be bathed in praise

How can throats but celebrate?

For there are
Waterfalls shouting
Thunderclouds clapping
Tidal waves laughing
Lightning bells ringing
Yet the one who has a concert for a world
Has sat patiently to hear
Our tiny tongues singing
That "Thou art great"

How can our tongues but celebrate?

The mind that has stored
All our violent words`
All our throats lying chords
Has decided to bear us in mind once more
And is excited as He
Intently stares
At the pleas of our
Weakest prayers
How can words but bellow out like flame

How can we but celebrate?

God's inked finger
Is writing on the walls
Inside our cheeks
As mortals stand and speak

YHWH's mouth
Is opened tall
Listen and be in awe
For the galaxy is starting to communicate
And the dust of man
Has begun to revelate

How can we but celebrate?

Let bodies quake
As God's mighty foot lands
In this place
Let arms be raised
As stars fall to join
This band of praise
    Let tongues be loose
        Let hearts beat loud
            Let our cymbal hands clap
                As Hosanna comes down
Let our bodies be sacrificed
In this cross-marching parade

How can we but worship?

How can we but celebrate?

EXCOMMUNICATION

Creation was words before it was earth and sky
Spoken construction created by
Tongue flung hammers
Jammed into rows of enamel nails
Rammed by blows through two panels of two by
fours
Forerunning the forests
Preceding the trees
Foregoing the gulfs
Predating our predecessors
The earth was in quake and speech was its epicenter

Strung together words
Sung from heaven's perch
An unknown language speaking a universe into birth
The vocabulary of formation
Nature's first verse

Seed planted vowels
Buried in chanted nouns
Enchanted consonants
Implanted continents
Third person subjects with
Confirmed predicates
"It is good"
The affirmed sentence

With terms He sent His semblance
Spoke His essence into presence

The entrance of presents, the exit of severance
Creation accepted the precepts of His utterance
In the utter annunciation of His fertile discussions
The discovery of humanity, the need for penance
"It is very good"
A life sentence

Words created creation with the intent of good
Creation berated the words
By doing not what they should
The Creator paraded creation
Out of the word rooted woods
Now all creation is gated and the Word is
Misunderstood

Exiting conversation's commune
First extracted from communication
Then excluded from communion
Excommunication

Those ancient words that animated sand to man
An initial conversation with uncreated tomorrow
The first solo song, unwritten monologue
They grow louder in our mother's womb
The dirt of our conception
The garden of our groom
A concept rises in concert
Concentrating its sound through centuries of trees
Generations of streams, decades of seas
Eden screams

Her labor pains, her exaction
Her beckoning, her contractions
Her water breaks, her reaction
Her sea section, her extraction
Her christening, her transaction
Her betrothal, her attraction

Infants of the garden
You hardened orphans of the tree
You were born of an Artist
Spoken poetry

Hear the singing soil, every gene is His
Skin made through sentences, our genesis
Now in our womb we must toil
From our origin we exited
The fabled hidden grove
Children of the exodus

I DO

My undying bride
I've memorized
The night of our covenant
The day of our betrothal
You walked down the aisle
Full of faith
Null of blame
You even fell to your face
As you approached the alter
Faltering not
But altering your approach
Not above reproach
But not wanting to encroach too
Quickly upon the beauty of our matrimony
The ceremony felt so natural
The presiding night sky officiated the proceedings
The assembly dressed finely as the shore
And shone as distant suns
I wrote my vows on the numberless stars
And countless sands
Placing on hands, a token of flesh
Our rings of a certain size – our offering
The twilight minister opened His mouth
"Do you solemnly swear to
Carry this covenant
To be one –
A people and a Father
A breath and a life
A keeper and a follower

A husband and a wife
Through toils and strife and unseen infidelities
To lands of fornication
Distant nations of adultery
Do you solemnly swear
To follow each other there?"
We declare, "I do"

Oh bride of the garden
I made a promise
To be your God
And make you My goddess
You ask in your shame
"Will He love me the same
Though I've been untrue?
Will He give me His name?"
I will and I do

You turned to me
Our consummation consumed
A nation's army in its depth
Our honeymoon stepped through death
To life on dry ground
Our pledge plodded into the promised land
We prodded prodigal man's riches into our clutches
Our love was a prodigy
None could understand, but began
Prompting trials through the judges
Our journey became a chronic chronicle
Of packing and unpacking luggage
When you endured pain's touches and the way was

Obscured, My strength allured you, but
When your wealth was assured and your boarders
Secured, you were lured away from me into idolatry
    Lusting after kings
    Undressing for gold
    Bearing your chest
    Opening your legs
    For a foreign guest
I witnessed it all
You sprawled out for
Other gods
Other lovers
Other frauds
Running from
Bed to bed
Land to land
Man to man
God to god
Snare to snare
You ask me, "Do you dare follow me there?"
I declare, "I do"

Oh bride of the garden
I made a promise
To be your God
And make you My goddess
You ask in your shame
"Will He love me the same
Though I've been untrue?
Will He give me His name?"
I will and I do

You returned to Me
We turned to building our dream home
Roamed from Bethel
Head stones turned to corners and pillows to a temple
Our abode was restful
Yet we began to wrestle
I guess that's why I call you Israel
For our love is a struggle
You smuggled other lovers into our humble home
Dressing them up in my clothes –
I'm pacified
It was all too real
But you both faked it –
You're gratified
Selling yourself to the highest bidder –
Classifieds
I longed for intimacy, but you were already
Satisfied
You ratified your dressed up harlots
    Calling them
        Praise and worship
        Religious equipment
        Dogmatic enlistment
    Naming them worthy of My name's employment
You ran after creeds and security
Doctrines and rigidity
Rigidly quoting your prayers
You ask me, "Do you dare follow me there?"
I declare, "I do"

Oh bride of the garden
I made a promise
To be your God
And make you My goddess
You ask in your shame
"Will He love me the same
Though I've been untrue?
Will He give me His name?"
I will and I do

You returned to Me
I poured out My blessings equally
Across your blessed curves and deformed torso
I took you home, leveling hills and valleys
So none were more so
Morsels I gave you as morals – just right
Never too little or more than enough
But My portions were never enough
You forced out equality
For four course blessings
Enforced poverty
Building fraudulently endorsed armories
Outsourced charity for horse drawn chariots
You traded the poor
Trained for war
Strained for glory
Abstained from My adoring
Pouring yourself into riches
Adorning yourself with splendor
Abhorring My selfless wishes
Ignoring your rewarding as My heir

You ask me, "Do you dare follow me there?"
I declare, "I do"

Oh bride of the garden
I made a promise
To be your God
And make you My goddess
You ask in your shame
"Will He love me the same
Though I've been untrue?
Will He give me His name?"
I will and I do

JEREMIAH 7

Hear the word, of the Lord all you
citizens of the sitting lineage.
Listen, all you Christians of the fitting in traditions,
for the Lord has spoken.
Open your ears, My heathens!

Pay attention
to the condition
of your religion
that has taken position
over your mission
as My children.

Your buildings are rebuilding a nation of sedation,
sedimentary demonstrations of comfortable
admiration.
A civilization of neglected realizations,
neglecting to realize that all your worship's
comprising
is the disgusting disguising of your
commitment's demising.
I brought you out of sin
with the blood on My Son's skin.
Again and again you sought Him to restore ya,
but your likeness is like that of Sodom and Gomorrah.

I've had My fill of your songs.
I long for your hearts.
I find no thrill in belonging

to the screen art
backlighting your hymns.
My ears rise to the brim with promises,
but I want your bodies' sacrifices.
My eyes are blind with churches –
all the same – no revolutionary versions.
Your Sundays are a burden.
You hide behind the blurred curtain
of worship and feel certain
that your prayers, songs, and sermons
will be heard,
thinking maybe I preferred
your words instead of your person;
but your blurred worship is persistent.
My gates are bombarded with identical prayers.
My courts are crowded with stares at a preacher.
My temple is littered with millions of teachers
teaching that song leading, table serving, and pulpit
speaking are what I care about.
But I want you when wanting Me
Isn't what everyone else cares about.

Oh my Christians!
When did Christ become a figurehead
instead of a commission?
When did My Son become flatbread
instead of a mission?
When did His blood become imbedded in dead
prayers instead of spreading you into submission?
When did His cross become printed on thread
instead of imprinted on your vision?

You're missing the point if
attending, seating, listening, and repeating
is the joint effort of your
effortless anointing.
I don't want to disappoint
all those who thought
getting baptized and being churched
would comprise the proper work to prove your worth.
But I have searched the earth
and when you're not hiding in your Sunday shirt
or your Wednesday skirt
you look the same as every unconverted
person who flirts with the comforts of
selfishness and inverted shame.
It does not matter if you claim My name
for the fact of the matter is
you all look the same –
the pagans, the Christians,
the tainted, the sinless,
the saved and the sinners,
the saints and imprisoned.

You are in prison,
My children.
Your comfort is your bars.
Your traditions are your cells.
Your boredom is your punishment
and your minds are your jails.
But don't you remember?
I freed you with nails,

broke the bars, opened the cells.
But you still sit in your chains,
spend your days lying in open graves.
I raised you from death but you still live the same
way.

Oh my unfaithful bride!
I loved you before time began to wind.
Behind your creation are lifetimes of preparation,
I created you to be Mine.
From the Egyptians, I saved you.
I kept you in mind.
From your hypocrisy, I braved your
commitment's decline.
I traded the life of the divine
for the strife of the slave.
I stayed by your side when you punctured mine,
sent me to the grave.
I forgave you and your kind,
generation after generation generating the same
replays.
And today you
slay Me still.
Your lips lie with what they say.
Your tongue deceives with great skill.
You fill pews to prove what your life fails to.
Do something more than just sit still!
You kill Me again
when you refuse to begin
living life as I did
when I lived

My life with you.
There will be no redemption for you
if you do not do as I implore you.

But don't doubt that I adore you.
Our reunion is overdue.
I long to restore you,
create something more for you,
relate to your core
and not just your core values.
For you are more valuable to Me than
doctrines, statements, or creeds.
Your faith in Me means more than
verses or beliefs,
attendance or deeds.
Whether you fail or succeed
I will speed to your every need.
Just please
stop all the pretending.
Stop using Me for salvation and
on it start depending.
Stop lending Me an hour a week,
and hourlessly – when your weak –
start spending hours on your knees.
Take My power to the streets.
Heal and nourish the least.
Bless every enemy.
And know
that as long as you are loving them and loving Me,
there is nothing else I could ever seek.

Hear the word of the Lord, all you
citizens of the sitting lineage.
Listen, all you Christians of the fitting in traditions,
for the Lord has spoken.
Open your ears.
For this message has not been spoken for years.
And if you miss it when it's this clear
and just let it disappear,
what will be your excuse when you've learned that
God's word was sincere?

RETURN RETURN

boom clap clap

return return

this inconsistent rhythm delivers the dissonance I
wrestle with through the pounding feet and clapping
palms of an out of step race

that's skin-covered bone-laden muscle-jointing soul-
bearing race we call human and we march to the beat
that doesn't sound right just

left-right-left-right-wrong-write-song-bout-left-and-
gone-right-to-fight-what's-left-from-right-that-on-
and-on-sight

return return

we slithered east from Eden's bride defying our
natural habitat of leaf and vine for human sacrifices
and crying blood bloodied sacrifices never human
always divine

we are the cities of Cain building vertically our
offerings of canned vegetables much like the upward
scale of cannibalistic unmentionables whose flesh
feeds corruption's mouth

return return

to the first booming clap of clapping plans

boom clap clap

cries the scraps of lands

return return

we are the green movement who farms amnesia
gardens forsaking the beds on which the heavens
used to plough

now we clash with creation like these stomps with
my sounds because we all live like we won't be kept
by the grounds like we aren't slaves to our own
hands

boom clap clap

cries the scraps of lands

return return

weeping widows of soil and sun heaving limbs on un-
cursed figs uncured predicament predicative
predictions of what would have been "In the
beginning"

if had only listened to the booming clap of clapping
demands

boom clap clap

cries the scraps of lands

boom clap clap

cries the scraps of lands

boom clap clap

cries the scraps of lands

boom clap clap

return return

to beginning's design cries the inevitably forgettable
regrettably inevitable grave never benign – rewind

boom clap clap

return return

to the tree to forbid yourself of bitten fruit fast and
feast on the afterbirth of your aborted self-
inseminated root – reboot

boom clap clap

return return

to the dust eat and be filled as the serpent crawl
through the wombs and tombs you circumvent –
rework it

boom clap clap

re re return

we we we were

out of step with natures metronome who clicks
one
two
three
four
five
six
then rests on the seventh

boom clap clap

return return

OH GOD! (PSLAMS 61 & 13)
A poem for two voices

(61 & 13)
Oh God!

(61)
My body crumbles before You
My crying and bumbling pour out like waves
Bowing as shores do
I lap up oceans of gasoline
Seas of kerosene
Transforming words into sparks
Thus igniting a beacon of faith in the dark
May I be aromatic as You listen
To my enigmatic transmission
My tongue burns as incense, rolling in
My mouth's insisting wet blanket
Making unmentionable motions
I'm blowing smoke

(13)
You hold me like water
In open hands rushing
Endlessly down the channeled beds in
Your palms, watering the garden of Your amnesia
Your hands have undergone anesthesia
You prolong my pain
Refusing to seize me as skeptic
Refusing to provide antiseptic

To my wounds
I sing the right tunes
Countless sins I refuse
Abstaining from booze, drugs, and tattoos
Yet You leave no clues
Of Your existence
This is my last prayer of insistence
That You break through the mystics
Or my persistent prayers
And distant stares
Will no longer employ this body's assistance
Sometimes I forget that
I'm just blowing

Smoke

Out the chimney in the house of Your trinket
May my exhalations be fragrant
Naked You see me
So no amount of promising
Could instill in You a favoring
Instead You need
Only my vow to be
Betrothed to You now
Bowing in my infancy
Cowering at Your infinite affinity for a recanting truth
For I can't see where lying
While lying at Your feet has gotten me to
Flagrant oaths be forgotten
A vagrant's home like a promise
It won't keep

Long

Enough I've waited
Craning my neck
Crinkling my eyes
But Your disguise of darkness
The four-wall lies of Your existence
This fiction religion of Your insistence
This long distance adoption from an unseen Father
This emptiness I auction off
To the highest bidding caller
No longer will I bear the weight of Your silence
I can't stand to wait for You
To revel Yourself to retracted eyelids
I can't keep on chanting a song
About a God to whom I belong
If You can't give up a breath, sigh, or yawn
For me to hold on
Much like a life that has done no wrong
Such innocence
Won't keep

Long

Is the empty wall between Your lips
And Earth's puckered kiss
But no distance can provide sufficient resistance
To the ballistic sound of my crying enlistment
Into the ranks of Your ears
Years may pass without one hint of Your existence
But relentless to adore You

Relentlessly I'll endure Your silence
Twilight messages I'll massage
Out of the passages of my mouth
Spouted out incantations
Blessed by my tongue's demands
Pressed into hands, whispered into breaths
And blown to the wind

When will my head and heart
Brain and bowels
Intelligence and emotion
Stop wresting with the fact that the words
Whispered within the rounds of hopeful prayers
And disappointed stares at an invisible, in-
visitable Friend are simply
Blown to the wind

Day after day sorrow borrows hope from tomorrow
and the rays of today's interest swelter the shade
But You are my shelter | And I have no shelter

For Your sake I forsake all foreign foretastes
Of dangers forebaders
For in You and Your name lies a fortune of fortitude
I'm fortified in forgiveness
Forged in Your form
The foreman of forever

I'm burning

My eyes at the wick
Last ditch seers
Wax tipped tears melting
Cylinders of hope – self-devouring
Betrothed to the smoke of my incinerated dowry

Hourly
I crawl to You
I weep on our bed of vows
Wetting the feathered pillows of Your wings
Covered by steel sheets on a metal mattress
My Master, Mistress, and Fortress
I rest on

You

Hide in darkness
Enlighten my eyes
Give light to disguise
Make light of the lies of Your silence
Look on me
And

Answer

My one request:
Arrest my life in Your love
Resist the death in me today
To live another one
That for the rest of my days
I may quest to sing the praise of

Your name

Is poison on my lips
Though it slays me I will continue to sip
The farther You hide, the deeper I drink
The darker my eyes, the longer I sink
Into the death of our life together

For Your love is never failing
And this affair keeps me
Ever wailing

Amen

UNITY

One mountainous olive night, I heard a hope song pour out like sweat drops of blood upon a martyr's thorny brow; who knew the last wish of a dying Son would be to make one where He found two, and to undo the endless multiplication of multiple denominations, creating crippled factorizations from fractions of a people, like a pinkie faction who claims control of the whole person's actions?

One rung the bell for all to be one called unity, where you and me find harmony in between the endless schemes of differing things we may see as disjointing because we all just need the same blood stained tree.

As I stood listening to my Savior's forgotten prayer, all the religious buildings started to stare, and the steeples raised their voices, and the church bells rang their noises, and the marquees raved their choices; they all sang to me the same song just in different keys, and the dissonating made me dizzy.

Soon the flickering lights gave way to dissipating sights.

I laid down, flat and fetal, on the old wooden road

And I dreamed.

I saw sick congregants congregating for remedies, found feigning family values refraining from mansions, now meeting in meager houses; the church took up its spouses on street corners, adorning the mourning with a unified message of hope, found fellowshipping in the cozy cushions of hearts where there is never a need for a bigger building or budget because love can house the universe.

I saw these forsaken fortitudes of mistaken platitudes transformed into real houses of praise – now used for homeless shelters, adoption centers, rehabilitation clinics, food pantries, and art galleries filled with interracial paintings of full circle peace signs.

I saw denominational marquees reprieved and their metal was beat into ploughs and trowels for the new compost garden out back.

I saw bullion laid communion trays shipped off to Cash for Gold to get appraised, and the money raised went to buy bread and wine for the lame and blind – they called that night their first Lord's Supper.

I saw a body that convinced unbelieving eyes, but not by cleverly clad, argumental sentiments or intellectually gad, doctrinal prods seeking tenements, but by their meagerly glad, confessional, intimate love for one another.

I saw millions raised for a building used for dying civilians instead of a youth pavilion.

I saw apostles admitting apostasy to their 1-800 hot lines and 4 digit prisons, found spitting the Spirit's salve into mud, mixing the medicine for Messianic blind-better-cream – free of charge and free of commitment.

I saw prophets prodding the pockets of suburbanite nonsense spending, redistributing lending to oppressed widows with widowed orphans, collecting widower tears in clear cherry jam jars, taking them one by one to the pearly gates of partiality parliament, slowly building a monument for begotten change like a new Vietnam Memorial of forgotten names.

I saw evangelists being Jesus instead of selling salvation and telling everyone how to be the church instead of which church to go to.

I saw pastors shepherding the wounded sheep instead of bickering over budgets.

I saw teachers enlightening minds at Starbucks and standing up in movie theatres to speak to crying souls.

I saw people worshiping God instead of worshiping with or without instruments.

I saw church attendance signs replaced with mirrors so we could all be reminded of what the church really is.

I saw stained glass windows shattered to make room for more doors.

I saw communion tables standing outside expensive restaurants, reminding everyone of the price He paid for our ultimate, forgotten feast.

And I saw the face of Jesus contently contained upon each and every set of eyes who accepted me just as I am, and upon every tongue that urged me to become holy like my God.

I saw unity in the body of Christ.

And then I woke up

I felt the warm-skin tenderness of Christ's body, though tired and torn, broken and worn, aborted yet perpetually born.

I was swept up into this dream that I know can be our present reality because I've seen what this body was given to achieve.

So with you by my side reaching into His, together we may die to what "church" is.

Now we have the opportunity to be broken on that olden tree, like the given Son did when he said that it was done.

And I know what we have to do in order to reach that communal feast:

We must break our bodies to
        Pieces to bring the
                Pieces of His body to
                        Peace.

I REMEMBER

I remember

I remember
who we were before this moment

I remember
the shadow of ourselves
now overshadowed by
the shelves
on which we placed
our former selves

I remember
how each of us here
placed our past
in tears
upon tiers of them
never to be touched again

I remember
how we approached God
hands empty
plans empty
demands empty
like we're supposed to be
emptying ourselves
upon those shelves
of our lives preceding
this moment

where, once and for all
we put to death our
superficial worshipping
and this
is its eulogy

remember with me

I remember
when God was idle
american made an
american idol
idly laid on hymn song titles
tidal waves of tidy Sunday
bridal singers
made their way to
display charades
we were all
masquerading
costume swingers
we
wore lips like
purists
but we were all
one day
tourists
of the
poorest Savior
sailing
war ships of
ignored trips

equipped with
bulletined
scripts
for this
event called
worship

I remember
what church used to be
sit, sing, sit, sip, sit, silent, sermon
exit
from a word prearranged
to a world unchanged
our despair unnamed
our problems deemed deranged
and we were estranged
in the exchange
of our time and expectations for
prewritten lines and explanations
about guys, whys, and places
that never addressed
our ache for a real God

I remember
when worship was a period of time
outlined by bulletins
bullied out by the
"not this again"
mentalities

I remember
when worship was protected
by walls and directions

I remember
the decorations
the song books
the screens
the long looks
at my jeans
the routines
the bowing
the closing
the opening
the spouting
off of words and notes
that never broke
through the wall
standing tall between
us and a God whose
reality we could never recall

I remember
it all

I remember
when worship was
contained by fear
constrained by years
of traditional rearing
rules never spoken

but somehow never broken
we were
token children
of an understood system
fearsome that we might become
too radical to
prevent our selfish intent

I remember
what worship was before this moment

I remember
how we were all under the persuasion
of evasion
evading any invasions
of commitment, discomfort, or costly
abrasions
we followed
the equation
me plus church minus cussing, sex, and alcohol
equals salvation

I remember
a time when I
would shout
"He is alive!"
and not one mouth
would scream
at the pronouncement
it seemed
no one

was out
but were streaming
back to their hiding places
where worship's
complacent
and singing's
accepted
and no one
is reckless
enough to stand
on the corner
or in the corner store
to sit with the homeless
or out their home's front door
and sing louder than the motor's roar
"how great is our God"

I remember
when all of us were frauds

I remember
when the only form of worship we knew
was what we did
following motions on motionless pews

I remember
when praise had nothing to do
with the other six days

I remember
When we forgot the sabbath was for resting
and the rest of the week
was for working

I remember
when the only service we worked
was the service in church
when worship that was pure
did not feed the poor
or
saw itself as the cure
or
cared for its enemy's needs more than yours
or
found the sick, dying, and lost and with them endured

I remember
when worship was a chore
when we all felt secure
just attending
but that was before

we realized
there is so much more
than pretending

but right now in this moment
as the saints are gathered round
and our God is present
and His Son takes precedent
and His Spirit's our resident
we are within the descent of the Triune
peasants in the tribunal land
and as we all stand
together repentant
grasping hands in our communal commitment to
clasping our plans to the eternal command
of what He meant for worship
and this is it
our opus
our openness
our hope is
our hopelessness
in everything we used to
hold as His
scope for what
worship is
worship is love

I remember
when He said
love is the opposite
of getting

but sacrificing everything
dying while living

I remember
when Jesus embodied it
His body embarked from
heavenly contentment
becoming this tent
of existence
God was a servant
the heavens observant
to humanity's torment
Creator tormented
creation tormentor
and that's the intent
of this event called worship
worship is a cross
worship is a loss
of everything that is not
embossed with the seal of God

but right now in this moment
and every moment hereafter
our praise of God will shake roofs and the rafters
our praise will be aloof from
the world and filled with laughter
our praise will ruthlessly pursue
a world filled with disaster
our praise will unashamedly
bear the proof of our master
for right here in this moment

and every moment hereafter
our praise will not be contained by
walls and churches
altar calls and holy perches
busy malls and facebook searches
school halls and worldly diversions

for our praise will bleed into all our excursions
it will break free from
stained glass
and
bible class
it will surpass
golden and brass
communion passing
trays to the next passive guest
it will clash
with standards
and traditions
for our praise
will live worship
as a mission

so right now in this moment
and every moment that proceeds
our praise will
flood the streets with song
shed blood for the needy and suffer along
give love to the enemy regardless of wrongs
place above ourselves the least of these
and with the weak be strong

for we will be the worshippers the Father seeks
and He will have to search for us no longer

for Father, we are Your worshipers
Your unworthy dancers
we are Your praisers
Your passionate romancers

and now we stand before you and say
"worship is not what we sing but how we obey"

and now we stand before you and say
"worship is not what we sing but how we obey"

and now we stand before you and say
"worship is not what we sing but how we obey"

and now we stand before you and say
"worship is not what we sing but how we obey"

I AM

Before florescent formations fomented
The foundations of your firmament
That is
Before the stars in your sky ever entered existence
Before light knew what bright meant
Before sky had a clue where up went
Before either were ever invented
I Am

Before terrestrial perennials terraced
Your planet's territorial terrain
That is
Before the plants on your ground were ever ordained
Before roots were ever arranged
Before fruit had a taste
Before either had a name
I Am

Before the ocean had a bowl
Before the surf discovered its roll
Before the grave was made Sheol
Before man had a soul
I Am

Before Eden was installed
Before the garden's serpent crawled
Before the tree, before the fall
I Am

For
I am truth before there ever could be false
I am perfection before there ever could be faults
I am by all
In all
Through all
All in all
And I am to be called
I Am

Before the curse usurped the ground and
Drove you away from the divine
Before you felt the separation between
Who you are and the intention of your design
Before you tried to abide in sources of
Death in order to find life
Before you combined yourself with any form of
Pleasure you could find
Before you felt so alone
Before you felt so dry
Before you tried to run away from My side
I Am
I am the vine

Before the cherubim ever guarded the garden
Before the flaming sword was ever sharpened
Before the chasm between God and man
Was ever widened
Before you lost all hope in becoming a
Citizen of heaven
Before all you earned was endless flame

Before all you deserved was righteous pain
Before you were a sheep hoping not just to be some
Lion's prey
Before you were a lost lamb longing for a pen
Longing to escape your fate
I Am
I am the gate

Before sustenance turned to gluttony and
Food was made an enemy
Before attraction was based in anatomy and
Sex was removed from matrimony
Before money became morality and
Greed grew into the only causality
Before you were empty without Me
Before you tried to satisfy your appetite with
anything
Before you strived to
Feel alive
By filling your strife
With the fleeting vices of
Your fleshly devices
Before your hunger for relief left pangs in your side
I Am
I am the bread of life

Before you ever became acquainted with pain and
death
Before you ever tasted loneliness
Before disease destroyed what you possess
Before eyes could be blind and ears could go deaf

Before you lost the ones you love to the
Grave's unyielding cleft
I Am
For before mankind stopped living
So that they might just survive
I am the resurrection and the life

Before that sadness that grips your mind
Led you to darkness and thoughts of suicide
Before that distortion of man hurt you
So that you now hurt yourself
Before you knew razors and wrists
Could create a new hell
Before wounds turned to scars
And scars became a way of life
I Am
I am the light

Before you even knew how to sin
I am where your salvation begins

Before you withdrew from the path of My way
Before you willfully and joyously disobeyed
Before you betrayed
The gift that I gave
Of that breath in your lungs
That life in your airways
By saying no to My love and yes to your heresy
Before you
Engaged with the enemy
Waged in sin with intensity

Before you
De-reigned My supremacy
Enflamed My jealousy
Before you chose
Greed over My adequacy
Lies over My accuracy
Pride over My advocacy
Before you chose your sinful self over Me
I Am
I am the Good Shepherd
Who lays down His life for His sheep

For before you were a spotted lamb
I Am

I am the way
Before you could ever run away from My call
I am the truth
Before you could ever walk away from My law
I am the life
Before you could ever turn away from My cross at
Golgotha's skull

So I beg you now
To withdraw

Withdraw from your sin
For I am your only temptation

Withdraw from your self
For I am making you a new creation

Withdraw from your pride
For I am ruining your reputation

Withdraw from self-righteousness
For I am your only mediation

Withdraw from your hopes and dreams
For I am your only expectation

Withdraw from your life
For I am your crucifixion

Before all time
I am all sufficient

Before all titles and designations
To My name all the cosmos listened

For

I am Jesus
I am the Word
I am Elohim
I am the Lord
I am the Christ
I am Messiah
I am Creator
I am Jehovah Jireh
I am the Lamb of God
I am Immanuel

I am the Begotten Son
I am Holy One of Israel
I am the Firstfruits
I am the Prince of Peace
I am the Bridegroom
I am the King of kings
I am the God of Abraham
I am the God of Jacob
I am the Alpha
I am the Omega

I am the Holy One worthy of praise
So withdraw unto My side
Withdraw and be made Mine
Withdraw and with Me stay
Withdraw into My way